CREATIVE WRITING JOURNAL

JULIAN FLANDERS

CREATIVE WRITING JOURNAL

Become the writer you want to be

SIRIUS

SIRIUS

This edition published in 2019 by Sirius Publishing, a division of
Arcturus Publishing Limited,
26/27 Bickels Yard, 151–153 Bermondsey Street,
London SE1 3HA

ISBN: 978-1-78950-013-4
AD006694US

Printed in China

Contents

Introduction

Although almost all writing can be described as "creative," for the purposes of this book we are going to concentrate on writing fiction. Creative writing—as opposed to academic and technical work—is the art of making up stories in order to share human experiences. A writer's purpose should be to come up with original, self-expressive, and entertaining words that, taken together, convey some kind of human truth. But where do you start? At the beginning, of course!

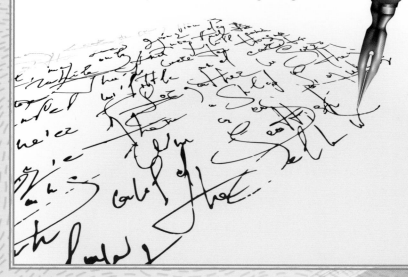

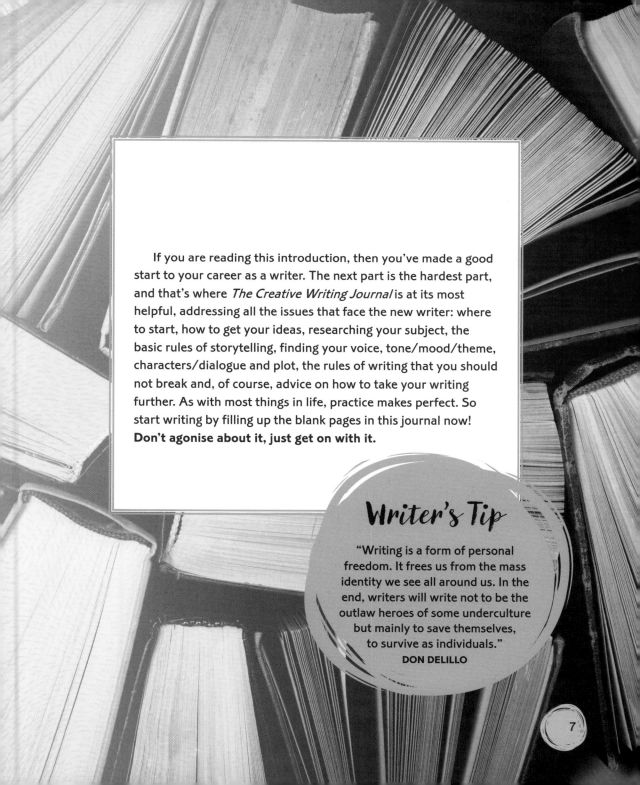

If you are reading this introduction, then you've made a good start to your career as a writer. The next part is the hardest part, and that's where *The Creative Writing Journal* is at its most helpful, addressing all the issues that face the new writer: where to start, how to get your ideas, researching your subject, the basic rules of storytelling, finding your voice, tone/mood/theme, characters/dialogue and plot, the rules of writing that you should not break and, of course, advice on how to take your writing further. As with most things in life, practice makes perfect. So start writing by filling up the blank pages in this journal now! **Don't agonise about it, just get on with it.**

Writer's Tip

"Writing is a form of personal freedom. It frees us from the mass identity we see all around us. In the end, writers will write not to be the outlaw heroes of some underculture but mainly to save themselves, to survive as individuals."
DON DELILLO

TOOLS OF THE TRADE

The list of things needed for the writer's toolkit is as long and complicated as you want it to be. In reality, there are no hard and fast rules, as everyone's needs and wants are different. However, you will definitely be able to sit down and write something if you are armed with the following tools:

- A computer with the relevant software, or a pen and paper if you feel more comfortable with those.
- A comfortable chair and a desk or table at the right height.
- A good dictionary.
- A grammar and style guide.

A good dictionary in indispensable, particularly since experience tells us that the spell-check function on your computer is not foolproof! Try the the *Merriam-Webster Dictionary*. For style guides, *The Chicago Manual of Style* is generally regarded as the standard work in the American publishing business. You may also choose to use a thesaurus, but beware of overusing it or your prose is certain to turn purple.

Of course, all these resources are available online, as are hundreds of apps aimed at the aspiring writer. These include story and plot generators, word selectors, time-management guides, finding words that rhyme and note takers, and there are even apps that vary the amount of light your computer generates to make sure you know what time of day it is! Some of them are free, and some are even useful: *Scrivener*, *Grammarly* and *Rough Draft* all come recommended, but apps that claim to help the creative process are probably best avoided.

Finally, you might find it useful to read some or all of the following: *Letters to a Young Writer* by Colum McCann, *Burning Down the House* by Charles Baxter, and *To Show and To Tell* by Phillip Lopate.

CHAPTER ONE

· ·

Where Do Ideas Come From?

Ideas Don't Grow On Trees

Evidence suggests that the biggest fear for aspiring writers attending their first creative writing class is the lack of a "big idea." Of course, having a big idea is great, but don't let the fact that you don't yet have one prevent you from attending a class. Ideas don't grow on trees, but just look around you and you'll soon find a subject!

Start with something simple. Write about a poster on the wall, describe your day, write about something that scares you or about someone you admire. If what you write isn't very good, then screw it up and put it in the trash or delete it, then start again. Although planning what you are going to write works for some people, many of the best ideas come from the act of writing itself. Get into the habit of it and your "big idea" might emerge spontaneously. Find out what time of the day is your most creative and give yourself a daily allowance of time or a target of a certain number of words. When you start out, write for yourself rather than for the approval of others.

EXERCISE: THE BIG IDEA

Write for 15 minutes on one of the following subjects:
• Describe someone who makes you angry. Explain how they make you feel and why.
• Or, finish the thought, "If I could change one thing about myself…."

Writer's Tip

"You get ideas from daydreaming. You get ideas from being bored. You get ideas all the time. The only difference between writers and other people is that we notice when we're doing it."
NEIL GAIMAN

Get Organized

Start making notes about any interesting stories you read in the newspapers or reliable news websites; go for a walk or a trip somewhere, then people-watch and imagine what their lives are like; listen to other people's conversations on the bus, **keep a journal, collect words, ideas and names, sounds, smells and other sensations, and jot down anything that piques your interest for some reason.** Some writers keep a notebook to hand at all times of the day and night. Of course, a phone is manna from heaven, both as a time-saver and as a multimedia tool for notes, recordings and photos.

Before you start your next writing session, ask yourself "what do I want to say?" and "how do I want to say it?", then jot down the "who, what, when, where, and how" of what you intend to write (see page 34). Use this information to structure your piece.

EXERCISE: 10-MINUTE BURST

Select an idea from your notebook or something that you heard or read about in the news recently. Use the space below to write in a 10-minute burst, without caring about the quality. After 10 minutes, review the material and use it to write a longer piece, for example 500 words, on the pages that follow.

Writer's Tip

"Always carry a notebook. And I mean always. The short-term memory only retains information for three minutes; unless it is committed to paper you can lose an idea for ever."

WILL SELF

CHAPTER TWO

· · · · · · · · · · · · · · · · ·

Write Now!

Find the Time

Don't be too disappointed if the first things you write are not as good as you hoped. You will get better with practice, so it's essential that you keep going and start to write regularly. A daily routine is best, so you need to be organized about it. Try setting yourself deadlines, in terms of time or the number of words you'd like to write. Aim high and you will achieve more, but don't attempt an epic novel or a family saga that encompasses five generations. Instead, write for 15 minutes during your lunch break, or 30 minutes on your commute to and from work.

EXERCISE: CLOCK WORK

Set a timer for 15 minutes and continue the following story: "It's not that way," said the man in the baseball cap. "It's over there." Stop writing when the bell goes.

Writing Skills Practice

Although we are going to concentrate on fiction, there is never a bad time to try some other form of writing, such as a blog, a poem (maybe a three-line haiku, or an Edward Lear-style limerick) or even a rap, just to get the juices flowing. But in terms of prose, you could start with some "flash fiction" (aka micro-fiction, sudden fiction or short-short stories). You could go for the six-word story (a good example of this would be **"For sale: baby shoes, never worn"**, as written by Ernest Hemingway), a Twitterature story 140 characters long (such as **"I opened the door to our flat and you were standing there, cleaver raised. Somehow you'd found out about the photos. My jaw hit the floor"** by Ian Rankin), the 50, the 100, the 150 or the "full monty" epic tale comprising 750 words.

EXERCISE: FLASH FICTION

Bearing in mind Mark Twain's assertion that "a successful story is not made up of what's in it, but what's left out of it," choose three different word counts (750 words or less) and write the following three short stories:
• A story from the point of view of someone much older than you.
• A story in which something important is lost.
• A story that involves a deep, dark fear.

The Facts of Fiction

Fiction can be defined as any form of narration that uses character, places, and events that are not necessarily factual. The five basic elements of fiction are character, plot, setting, theme, and style.

- Characters define "who."
- Plot determines "what."
- Setting establishes "when and where."
- The theme is a story's message or moral.
- Style explains "how," often using a particular narrative technique or point of view.

Remember to enjoy your writing sessions; think your wildest ideas and use your imagination to create your characters and the world in which they live. Try to create characters that you love or hate, stir some emotions and bring it all to life. When you have written something you are pleased with, read it out loud. You can read it to yourself first and then to your specially chosen first audience!

EXERCISE: WHO, WHAT, WHEN, WHERE AND HOW?

On the pages that follow, write one or two flash fiction pieces in which it will be hard to include all the "who, what, when, where and how" elements. If it helps, create a list of the elements of your story before you begin. You should follow the short pieces with some longer ones, incorporating all the basic elements and presenting them in the tone of your choice.

CHAPTER THREE

· · · · · · · · · · · · · · · · · · · ·

The Basic Rules
of Storytelling

We Are All Storytellers

Stories have been used to hand down learning and knowledge for thousands of years, by engaging our curiosity, emotions, and imagination. They still play a central part in our daily lives—in what we read to our children, in the anecdotes we share socially, in the books we read, and the films we watch. They are recognized as an important way to connect with any audience, and are increasingly used in the workplace, advertising, and fundraising. For Clare Patey, Director of the Empathy Museum, the reason is obvious: **"Stories are the way we understand and make sense of the world we find ourselves in."**

EXERCISE: CONVEYING EMOTIONS

Write about an event in your life that made you feel a certain way. The aim of your piece should be to prompt the same feeling in your readers. Read it aloud to a friend, colleague or member of your family. Ask what feelings it aroused in them.

The Seven Basic Plots

*I*n 2004, the journalist and writer Christopher Booker published a list of what he saw as the seven basic plots of all stories. Although his was not an original thought, his wording suggests the following themes: **overcoming the monster; rags to riches; the quest; voyage and return; comedy; tragedy; rebirth—often splashed with a liberal dab of romance.** Another theory says that there are seven themes in fiction: **love, money, power, revenge, survival, glory, and self-awareness.** Think about the stories you have read and written so far, and see whether they fit into any of these categories. The chances are that they do.

Luckily for all would-be writers, most stories have more than one theme, and it is the superimposition of these themes, with the arising conflicts between the characters concerned, that makes a story interesting.

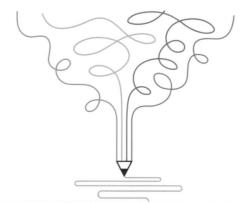

EXERCISE: THE TRIPLE-O PLOT

Choose a book you are familiar with. Try to identify the plot ("a detailed scenario of what makes up the story") by noting its "objective," the "obstacles" that get in the way and the eventual "outcome."

Top 10 Rules of Storytelling

1 Show, not tell.
"Telling" is brief, factual, and cold, whereas "showing" is detailed, human, and communicative—it adds drama and can stir the heart.

2 Try to create characters that people are going to like.
The film company Pixar explains in its "22 Rules for Storytelling" that the audience admires characters for trying rather than for their success. In other words, it's always more about the characters' journey than it is their actual destination. An appealing character would most likely be an underdog with the sort of faults we all think we have.

3 Try writing about an event in your life that made you feel a certain way.
Your aim should be to write it in such a way that your readers will experience the same feeling.

4 Stories need a beginning, a middle, and an end.

5 Stories need to be aimed at everyone.
Good stories need to be inclusive, so write for your readers and give them something to identify with.

6 Give your story a clear structure and purpose.
Try using the Story Spine, a technique used in improvisational theatrical performance, created in 1991 by teacher and author Kenn Adams:
- Once upon a time there was … (introducing the story).
- Every day … (the main character's routine is established).
- But one day … (the event occurs as the main character breaks the routine).
- Because of that … (there are dire consequences).

- Because of that ... (doubts begin to creep in).
- Until finally ... (the climax: success/sometimes failure).
- Ever since then ... (the resolution and the moral of the story).

7 Focus your story on its main point.
Make sure the plot is easy to understand and that the language matches the subject matter.

8 Great stories appeal to our emotions.
Make use of the six basic emotions: anger, disgust, fear, happiness, sadness, and surprise, to make your readers laugh, cry, love or hate.

9 Misdirect your readers.
Read your story, imagine in which direction it seems to be going, then move the narrative in the opposite direction. Good use of dead ends and red herrings (plotlines that looks like there're going somewhere, but really aren't) can lull the reader into thinking they know what's going to happen. You can then deliberately undermine that notion.

10 Don't wait until you've written everything else to write the ending. Work it out early and it'll help you put all the pieces together.

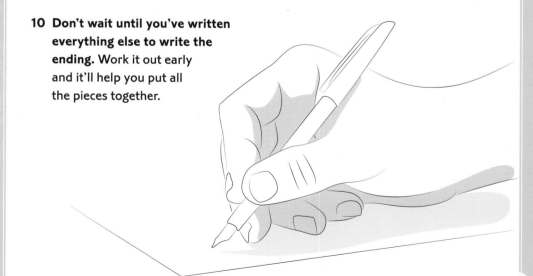

EXERCISE: THE STORY SPINE

Spend some time coming up with some characters, a plot and a setting. Using this information, fill in the story spine skeleton. When you've done that, flesh out the story using as many of the techniques discussed in this chapter as you can.

Writer's Tip

"Don't tell me the moon is shining. Show me the glint of light on broken glass."
ANTON CHEKHOV

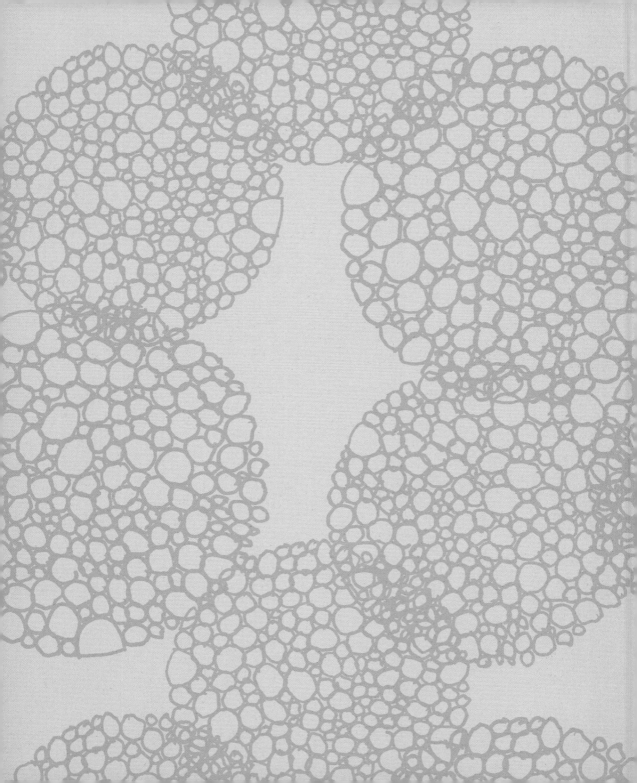

CHAPTER FOUR

· ·

Behind the Scenes

Researching Your Subject

Whether you are writing fiction or non-fiction, research will be a fundamental part of your work. Of course, **the amount of research will vary according to your subject**, but it will always be time-consuming. However, researching a subject can also be fascinating, and it will help the writing process immensely and ensure that you avoid making the kinds of errors that will put readers off your work. For non-fiction, your research will most likely provide the actual basis of your writing. If your work has an historical setting, involves police work or relates to military subjects, medical matters or science fiction, for example, then your workload will also be heavy. It will be up to you to find the right balance between factual accuracy and the creative demands of the story—but take great care to get it right!

EXERCISE: HOW DO THEY DO IT?

Research a profession—for example, a car mechanic, a dog trainer, a ballerina—and write a page of notes about it. Then imagine a character who does this job and write a paragraph or two about them, incorporating some of this information.

Be Organized

Start with some lists: what are your areas of interest? What specific topics will you need to cover? Identify how much time per day or per week you are prepared to set aside for research, get on the internet and make a list of books that will be useful for your work, think about anyone you would like to interview, and identify any trips that you'd be prepared (or can afford) to make in search of first-hand information.

Of course, there's no point in collecting hundreds of bits of paper and other notes only to create a disorganized mess that you won't be able to access later. You need to decide what works best for you: perhaps a notebook, some files, and a pin board. Or you may prefer a digital system, such as *Evernote* or *Scrivener*. Make a note of all helpful website addresses, phone numbers, book references, and so on, as there is nothing worse than unearthing a golden nugget of information essential for your plot, only to forget where you found it.

Resources

Museums are a treasure trove of historical, scientific, artistic, and cultural interest, so make the most of your visits. Most do not allow flash photography or phones, so take a notebook or a hand-held recorder. Ask questions of the tour guides or exhibition staff if there is anything extra that you want to know—very often they are experts in their field and are only too pleased to show off their knowledge. Many museums hold events such as lectures, workshops, and talks that might be relevant to your area of interest. They are likely to be free or cheap to attend, so make sure you search out their listings.

The **internet** is now the world's greatest research tool, but you must use it carefully. For every reputable website, there are many that contain outdated and even false information. With experience, you should be able to recognize legitimate and trustworthy sites. Good places to start include *Wikipedia* (including the citations and references at the bottom of each

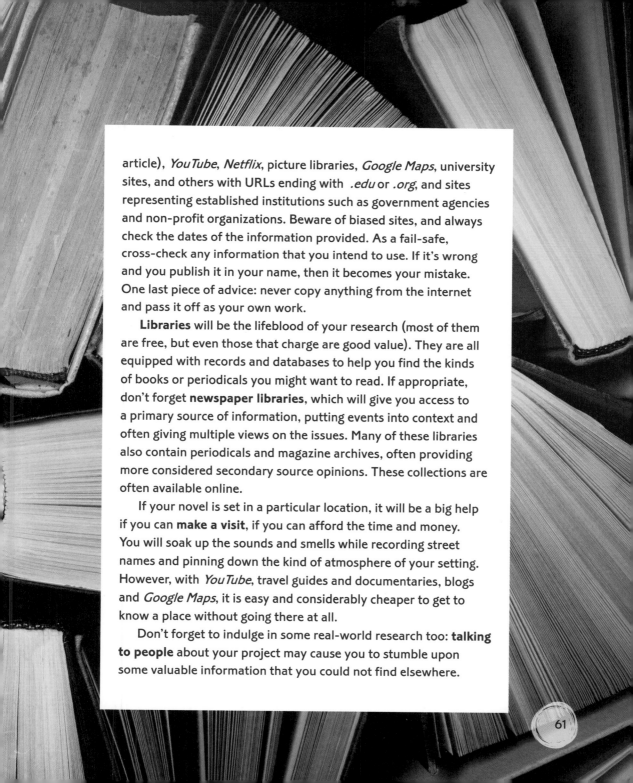

article), *YouTube*, *Netflix*, picture libraries, *Google Maps*, university sites, and others with URLs ending with *.edu* or *.org*, and sites representing established institutions such as government agencies and non-profit organizations. Beware of biased sites, and always check the dates of the information provided. As a fail-safe, cross-check any information that you intend to use. If it's wrong and you publish it in your name, then it becomes your mistake. One last piece of advice: never copy anything from the internet and pass it off as your own work.

Libraries will be the lifeblood of your research (most of them are free, but even those that charge are good value). They are all equipped with records and databases to help you find the kinds of books or periodicals you might want to read. If appropriate, don't forget **newspaper libraries**, which will give you access to a primary source of information, putting events into context and often giving multiple views on the issues. Many of these libraries also contain periodicals and magazine archives, often providing more considered secondary source opinions. These collections are often available online.

If your novel is set in a particular location, it will be a big help if you can **make a visit**, if you can afford the time and money. You will soak up the sounds and smells while recording street names and pinning down the kind of atmosphere of your setting. However, with *YouTube*, travel guides and documentaries, blogs and *Google Maps*, it is easy and considerably cheaper to get to know a place without going there at all.

Don't forget to indulge in some real-world research too: **talking to people** about your project may cause you to stumble upon some valuable information that you could not find elsewhere.

EXERCISE: WORK BACKWARD

Imagine you are about to write one of your best-loved novels. Start by making some lists: who are the characters, why is the story worth telling, how will you reach the resolution? Then write down the "where" and "when" of the story in the form of an outline, and list the research resources you might require to source the necessary information.

When to Stop Research and Start Writing

There is no doubt that you will enjoy your research, but at some point you will have to stop researching and start writing! It can be difficult to decide when that point comes, as there is no way of knowing when you are completely ready to write. Some writers research a certain subject and then write some scenes or events around it before researching something else. This keeps you moving forward and provides a kind of balance between input and output. Another useful tool would be to set a date by which you must start writing, then work backward, allotting yourself a certain amount of time for research. You can always do additional research as you write, but at least you will have got your story underway.

Having put so much time and effort into research, it is tempting to try to squeeze every last detail you have researched into your text. This is dangerous, however, as your prose might start to resemble a textbook. Use detailed information by all means, but only when it's useful—to give context or to move the story on, for example. Narrative comes first; use research to bring your story to life.

Don't forget to credit everyone who has helped you along the way in your research.

EXERCISE: STOPPING AND STARTING

Carrying on from the exercise on page 62, it is helpful to know when to finish researching and start writing. Try the following two activities:
• Choose a particular scene or passage from your best-loved book, and write down—in detail—what you would need to know before you begin writing. Try to estimate how long that would take you.
• Write an outline synopsis of the book, then create a "mind map" of the story. To do this, write an index card for each scene and then set the cards out on the floor, making sure there are no plot holes. Then try swapping them around to see if you could make the story even more exciting.

CHAPTER FIVE

· · · · · · · · · · · · · · · · · · · ·

Tone, Mood, and Theme

Tone

Tone in writing is much the same as tone in music and speech, both of which are more immediately recognized. "Don't take that tone with me!" is a sentence that we have all heard and instantly understood at some time in our lives. Without the inflection of the speaker, however, it is a lot less effective. A good example is to think about times you have emailed or texted someone while meaning one thing, but the person took it to mean something else.

In writing, tone is actually a literary device that shows the attitude or approach the author takes toward the work's central theme—for example, humorous, solemn, distant, intimate, ironic, arrogant, condescending, sentimental, and so on. Any emotion that humans are capable of feeling can be an example of tone in literature. By choosing certain words (**diction**) and selecting particular sentence structures (**syntax**), writers can express thoughts and feelings that throw light on the personalities of their characters or even themselves.

TONE IN LITERATURE

Have a look at some of your best-loved books, read a passage or two and think of the sorts of words you can use to describe the tone of the passages you read. Here is an example to start you off:

"If you really want to hear about it, the first thing you'll probably want to know is where I was born, and what my lousy childhood was like, and how my parents were occupied and all before they had me, and all that David Copperfield kind of crap, but I don't feel like going into it, if you want to know the truth."

The Catcher in the Rye, J.D. SALINGER—an extract that can be interpreted as sarcastic, cynical, critical, disparaging, depressing or sad

How to Convey Tone in Your Writing

Tone is unlikely to remain the same throughout your story, but it is important that you find the **appropriate tone** for the scene you are writing, and make sure it is consistent, You can do this through **the words you choose,** or through **the length of your sentences.** For example, short sentences are great for fast or intense action, urgent situations or angry characters. However, an endless series of short sentences would eventually lose their effect, so make sure you insert longer sentences for slow action and to create calm or thoughtful moments in between. Romances tend to be more effusive and expressive, comedies more buoyant, and so on. Some writing guides suggest that if you're unsure about what tone to adopt for fiction, visualize the book as a film and imagine what emotions or feelings its musical soundtrack would convey.

Other devices you can use are **formal/informal language, conversational style, instilling energy through the rhythm of the words** and **using the imperative.** A wonderful idea is to **treat your subject in an unpredictable manner**—read Kurt Vonnegut's *Slaughterhouse-Five* or Jonathan Swift's *A Modest Proposal* for fine examples of this.

Remember, **"It's not what you say, it's how you say it."** Build tension through conflict, or write with forgiveness, understanding or humour. Use your own unique voice, because that's what the reader wants to hear.

EXERCISE: AN ANXIOUS DOG WALK

Take the following words: sadness, regret, courage, tension, sympathy, love/romance, happiness, pride, sarcastic, excitement, hate, fear, anxiety, nostalgia. Write a description of a dog walk in the park, conveying some of these attitudes. You don't need to use the words themselves in your piece.

Mood

Mood describes the feelings that words evoke in the reader. While tone and mood are distinct literary devices, they are closely related. For example, it's not unusual for a poem with a solemn tone to have a solemn mood, i.e. to make the reader feel solemn. Similarly, if an author wants to point the finger at a political issue, they might use a critical tone to create a mood of anger or outrage in their readers.

Most pieces of literature have a prevailing mood, and shifts in this mood may function as a counterpoint, provide comic relief, or echo the changing events in the plot. Every aspect of a piece of writing can influence its mood, from the setting, imagery, description, and the author's choice of words, through to the pace of the writing and its tone. For instance, a story that begins "It was a dark and stormy night" will most likely have a dark, ominous or suspenseful mood.

MOOD IN LITERATURE

Consider these two excerpts from the same book that evoke different moods:

(i) **"There was no moon, and everything beneath lay in misty darkness: not a light gleamed from any house, far or near all had been extinguished long ago: and those at Wuthering Heights were never visible..."**

(ii) **"Gimmerton chapel bells were still ringing; and the full, mellow flow of the beck in the valley came soothingly on the ear. It was a sweet substitute for the yet absent murmur of the summer foliage, which drowned that music about the Grange when the trees were in leaf."**

Wuthering Heights, EMILY BRONTË—(i) depressing; (ii) calm and peaceful.

How to Convey Mood in Your Writing

The time of day, season, weather, and **setting** can all influence the mood of a piece. Something as simple as moving from day to night can change the mood from safe to frightening. The key to using setting to create mood is to pay attention to the way your characters interact with what's going on around them. Are they challenged by the setting, or comforted? **Imagery**, too, plays a part in mood. Consider a building in an alleyway, with broken windows and hanging rafters, the alleyway littered with debris and shadowy figures, all pointing toward possible danger. The writer's **choice of words** is extremely important in setting mood. The **rhythm and pace of the sentences** will affect both tone and mood: short sentences create a feeling of haste, while long sentences full of commas can make the reader breathless and anxious. You can, of course, speed up your sentences and then slow them down, to vary the mood.

A writer can also use **dialogue** and **monologue** to support the atmosphere they want to create. Whether using light-hearted banter or heated accusations, just make sure that the characters involved are in tune with the atmosphere you are trying to create.

Another useful tool for evoking mood is **description**. The narrator, first person or otherwise, can decide what to focus on and what to ignore. For example, they could choose to describe a shattered porcelain baby doll in the gutter rather than the beautiful blue sky above.

EXERCISE: THE BARN

Most students who have done a creative writing course will be familiar with John Gardner's famous exercise for creating mood through description. This is a great exercise, but it is quite challenging. Give it a go and see what you come up with: in 250 words, describe a barn as seen by a man whose son has just been killed in a war. However, do not mention the son, or war, or death.

Theme

The theme of a literary work is what the story means, its "big idea," its pulse and the glue that binds it together. This is distinct from the work's subject, which will act as its foundation; the theme consists of the opinions expressed on the subject. For example, a writer may choose war as a subject for their story, but the theme of the story may be the opinion that "war is good for absolutely nothing."

For a story to be meaningful and have a lasting effect on the reader, it needs to have a theme. Themes are usually universal in nature, touching on the human experience and evoking emotion in the reader. A theme should be present in the pivotal plot elements, character development, and conflict resolution. For example, we might admire the main character for their strength or their ability to deal with adversity.

Stories can have more than one theme, although one is likely to be the major theme, with other minor themes around it. For example, Shakespeare's *King Lear* shines a light on **justice, reconciliation, madness, and betrayal**, while George Orwell's anti-utopian *Animal Farm* suggests that **absolute power corrupts and knowledge is power**.

Common themes in stories include: crime doesn't pay; we are our own worst enemies; coming of age; overcoming the odds; love conquers all; capitalism; betrayal; morality; prejudice; death; religion; good vs evil; war; religion, family, humanity vs nature; and the individual vs society.

It is important for new writers to realize that you don't have to search for a new or original theme, nor do you have to come up with a new one for each of your stories. Remember, **"It's not what you say, it's how you say it."**

THEME IN LITERATURE

"If he needs a million acres to make him feel rich, seems to me he needs it 'cause he feels awful poor inside hisself and if he's poor in hisself, there ain't no million acres gonna make him feel rich, an' maybe he's disappointed that nothin' he can do'll make him feel rich."

The Grapes of Wrath, JOHN STEINBECK—wealth, family, man's inhumanity to man

CREATING THEMES IN FICTION

Writers tend to develop their themes in two different ways. Some set out to explore all the themes they intend to use before they begin writing. Others might start with the main theme but leave minor themes to emerge for themselves, perhaps not even recognizing them until they review their work at the editing stage. They may then cut or add to the text to highlight the themes that have emerged. Decide which system works best for you.

Themes are not generally stated explicitly in the text and are usually suggested by actions; after all, people naturally express their ideas and feelings through their actions. **Authors can also put words into their characters' mouths**—most likely the main character's mouth—to develop a story's theme, presenting it through **thoughts and conversations**.

Writers also have literary devices to call upon to emphasize or hint at a work's underlying themes. They might use **symbols**, such as an object, person or place, to represent something else. For example, a storm may represent unrest and imminent danger, or the style of Luke Skywalker's clothes as opposed to Darth Vader's may represent the battle between good and evil. Writers may make use of **motifs**—elements that recur throughout a story to help reinforce its themes. For example, Shakespeare's use of dark and light in *Romeo and Juliet* is effectively employed to show the contradictory nature of love.

EXERCISE: ETHICAL WRESTLE

Some things in life are simple; others less so. For example, what should be done about a man who steals a loaf of bread to keep his family from starving? What about a woman who becomes a prostitute to keep her daughter safe? Think about an ethical issue that you wrestle with. Consider the different points of view and write 250 words on the issue, examining both sides of the argument.

CHAPTER SIX

. . . .

Character Development, Dialogue, Structure, and Plot

Character Development

Character development is a vital part of creative writing. Don't forget that a thrilling plot can be undermined by flat characters, while a mediocre plot can be brought to life by characters that the reader likes. Remember, too, that your task as a creative writer is not simply to think for a while and conjure up an imaginary person; it is also a matter of showing your readers how your character's persona develops during the course of the story. Even though your characters are fictional, they must be believable; and to be believable, they need to have depth.

EXTERNAL CHARACTERISTICS

With your main character, it will pay dividends for you to **build up a picture of them** at an early stage in your project. You should start by developing their external characteristics. You will need to **start a file** for this information—your character "bible"—much of which may not be used in your story, but will **inform the way your character thinks, acts, and reacts**. It is vital that you go into this in depth. You should include the following information:

- Basics: name, age, place of birth, nationality, education, occupation, and income.
- Physical appearance.
- Speech and style of communication.
- Style of dress.
- Health.
- Distinguishing features.
- Posture.

INTERNAL CHARACTERISTICS

An important tool to work on early is **establishing a backstory** for your character. We are all defined by our past experiences, and so is your character. To understand them fully, you have to understand them in the context of their lives. Motivation always comes from an amalgamation of past experiences. Even if you don't share it with your readers, you need to know what motivates them. It's like being told that someone you know but don't like behaves in a certain way because something devastating happened in their past. You suddenly feel better disposed toward them. A backstory makes it easier for the writer to hear the character's voice and sympathize with them. A timeline of their life might help you organize this information.

It is also essential to **establish your character's goals and motivations**. It is likely that your main character has a current goal, and that is why the story exists and why it has to be told now. It's what they want that drives the plot and propels them on their inner journey. For example, Harry Potter's goal is to defeat Lord Voldemort, while Hamlet's goal is to avenge his murdered father. Their motivations follow on from their goals: Harry Potter's is to avenge his family and ensure the safety of the wizarding world, while Hamlet wants to prove that he did not imagine his father's ghost and that he can make decisions.

No one is interested in a character for whom everything goes smoothly, so it is essential that the writer puts a few obstacles in their way.

CONFLICT IN FICTION

While developing your main character, it helps to decide who or what would be their most worthy adversary. It could be one of the following:

- **Character vs Character**: for example, Othello vs Iago.
- **Character vs Society**: for example, Winston Smith vs Big Brother in *1984.*
- **Character vs Nature**: for example, Captain Ahab vs Moby-Dick.
- **Character vs Technology**: for example, Victor Frankenstein vs Frankenstein's monster.
- **Character vs Supernatural**: for example, Jack Torrance vs The Overlook Hotel in *The Shining.*
- **Character vs Self**: for example, Jason Bourne or Bridget Jones.

DYNAMIC VS STATIC CHARACTERS

As we have already seen, good characters learn, develop, and change during the course of their story; these are known as "dynamic characters." They might make a conscious decision to change—like Mr Darcy in *Pride and Prejudice* for the sake of love, or Dr Jekyll, who is compelled to drink a serum and change into the evil Mr Hyde. But other characters undergo an internal journey and an adventure, yet finish exactly as they started. These are known as "static characters." Good examples of these would be Sherlock Holmes, or Katniss Everdeen in *The Hunger Games* trilogy. For Mr Holmes, his unchanging nature actually makes him a compelling character. For Katniss, however, it is her refusal to give up her core principles, despite the efforts of President Snow, that drives her to rebel against the state of Panem and the murderous games that it plays with the poor.

SECONDARY CHARACTERS

As well as a main character, most stories also include an antagonist, hopefully a villain who is complex and layered. It is essential for writers to spend a bit of time working on their secondary characters—friends and rivals, or even symbolic and non-human characters—who are essential in moving the story forward. A secondary character can also act in other ways. For example, Atticus Finch in *To Kill a Mockingbird* has a belief in justice, common sense, and wisdom. This belief acts as a kind of pillar around which Scout can develop from childhood innocence to a girl with a strong sense of right and wrong. You could also create a foil for your main character, whose contrasting qualities can highlight the main character's traits. Consider Dr Watson, for example, whose humanity is able to connect Sherlock Holmes to the real world in which he operates.

USE OF VOICE

In any book, an author will be working with their own voice, the main character's speaking voice and their internal voice, plus the voices of the secondary characters. That's a lot of voices! To get readers to believe in your story, the voices have to be consistent throughout. Consistency invokes trust. In a perfect world, your readers should be able to identify who is speaking without having a name explicitly attached.

We've already discussed how important a backstory is and how helpful it is to create a character study. Since a character's voice is largely defined by what they say to themselves, you can use these resources to create their thoughts. Like us, they are the result of their life experiences; for example, they might be humble, arrogant, sensitive or sarcastic.

In writing dialogue, it is important to remember that your characters probably don't speak like you do. Take some time to research how other people actually speak. Go and sit in a coffee shop, bar or restaurant. Take a notebook with you and do a bit of eavesdropping. Make notes on the kind of sentences you hear, the words used, and any idioms and slang. This will help you to create authentic dialogue. If you are writing an historical piece, read letters or other literature that was written at the time—y**ou can be sure that a 14-year-old Victorian girl would not sound like a member of the *Snapchat* generation** (see also page 110).

EXERCISE: FIND A VOICE

Chose a stereotypical character such as the drill sergeant, the self-obsessed prima donna, the hard-boiled detective, the mad scientist, and so on, and lock them in a room with no windows. Imagine what might happen: they'd be confused, worried, angry, scared, and bored. Then what? Use your imagination to work out what they'd do next, in 250 words. They might surprise you!

Dialogue

Dialogue is narrative conveyed through speech. The characters in a story may express themselves internally via thoughts or as a narrator, or they may do so externally through conversations and actions. After all, what people say and how they say it is an expression of their character. Word choice tells a reader a lot about a person, such as their appearance, ethnicity, sexuality, background, and morality. It can also tell the reader how the writer feels about them.

Dialogue is an extremely flexible tool—not only does it give insight into characterization, but it also conveys information, sets the scene, advances the action, creates character dynamics, conveys emotion, reminds the reader of anything important, and foreshadows future dramatic action. But you have to get it right! Although it does not have to be grammatically correct, dialogue should read like actual speech. You need to be selective, continually paying attention to word repetition, hesitation, stammers, polite conventions, and dead ends.

ESTABLISHING HOW EACH OF YOUR CHARACTERS TALK

How your character speaks will depend upon a number of factors: geographic background (a Texan doesn't speak in the same way as a Bostonian), educational level, age (like, is your character, like, a total teenager?), personality (is your character nervous, impulsive, aggressive, flirtatious, shy?), your character's relationship with the person they're talking to (their boss, friend or 5-year-old son), and your character's attitude to the conversation topic. Does it make them nervous, proud or defensive? Would they rather just avoid the subject altogether? Finally, of course, you need to be mindful of the time in history in which your story is set.

DIRECT AND INDIRECT SPEECH

Direct speech or dialogue is generally a conversation between two or more characters. This, however, is not always the most convincing and appropriate way of presenting a conversation, particularly as many conversations are rather boring when written out word-for-word. You could try adding some non-verbal details to the exchange, to create emotion and tension. For example:

"Hey, Joe."

Joe looked down, sticking the toe of his shoe into the loose earth.

"Hey yourself," he said, without looking up.

Sam immediately knew there was something wrong.

Alternatively, you could go for indirect speech, which does away with dialogue and relies instead on thoughts, memories or recollections of past conversations to convey important narrative details. Writers can also combine the two devices to increase the dramatic tension.

Rules for Writing Dialogue

- Keep sentences and conversations short, and cut out anything unnecessary. Allow gaps in the communication, and let the reader fill in the blanks.
- Make sure your characters sound different from each other. To achieve this, add some intrigue to the words—some banter or some slang.
- Avoid small talk, decide the outcome of each conversation, and end it as soon as the point is made.
- Avoid attributions ("he said," "she said") if at all possible.
- Get your punctuation right (inside the closing quote marks).
- Interrupting conversations is effective, as are characters who are thinking during the conversation and not quite engaging with the others involved.
- Use silences and changes of subject.
- Mix actions into the conversation.
- Be awkward, and answer a question with another question.
- Above all, keep it moving—fast.

EXERCISE: HE SAID, SHE SAID

Write a dialogue between three characters. It can be about anything you like, and should be at least six lines long. The only verb you can use is "said."
• Rewrite the dialogue using only descriptive verbs.
• Rewrite the dialogue without using attributions. Instead, let the reader know who is talking by including actions and descriptions of the characters.
• Lastly, rewrite your dialogue using whatever combination of tags and action you think will make it work best.

Structure and Plot

The **plot** is the series of **events that make up your story**, and includes the order of events and how they relate to each other. The **structure** (aka narrative structure) **deals with its mechanics**—how the chapters/scenes are broken up, what the conflict is, what the climax is, what form the resolution will take, and so on. While the plot is unique to your story, there are a number of common narrative structures to help you bolt it together. In a perfect world, all this would come to you in a flash of inspiration, but if that doesn't happen, you might find the following structures helpful.

Common Narrative Structures

There are many ways to structure a story. Knowing something about the ways stories are commonly structured will help you decide how you might move your plot forward.

The **Three-Act Structure** has a beginning, a middle, and an end. Simple and easy to understand, it is commonly used in stories, novels, and screenwriting today. The **Narrative Arc** takes the form of a pyramid. The story starts at the bottom left, introducing the characters and the setting. The action rises up the left-hand side of the pyramid through a series of events that complicate the story, increasing the drama and suspense. At the top is the climax, the showdown, where the characters meet the enemy and either win or lose. After this, the action falls away down the right-hand side of the pyramid through another series of events. At the bottom is the resolution (or denouement), in which the problems are resolved and the story ends.

Another model, suggested by the American author James Scott Bell, is **"a disturbance and two doorways through which there is no return."** The writer starts by introducing the characters, the setting and the status quo. They are all then compressed and hurled at speed through the first doorway. Once inside, a disturbance occurs—a late-night phone call with bad news, the sudden death of a relative, or an argument. It is always something that threatens the main character's way of life and forces them to exit through the second doorway in search of a resolution.

If your main character is stumbling into an unknown world—in fantasy or science fiction, for example—then the **Hero's Journey** might work well. The journey begins in the known world but our hero/heroine is soon called to adventure. A mentor may be needed to persuade them to accept this adventure, which they then do. As they enter the new world, they face trouble from an evil antagonist. Although they win in the end, during the conflict the hero experiences literal or figurative death before being reborn with a new view of the world. They strive to make up for past mistakes before returning to the world they once knew, and then live out their days.

A final example, **In Media Res** (Latin for "into the middle of things") refers to a plot that begins in the middle. Often used in thrillers and murder mysteries, the story—which starts as the killer turns away from their victim—is told in flashbacks or through conversation. The plot will still have an upward trajectory right from the start, in which essential background information is liberally sprinkled throughout—for example, the events that led up to the crime in the first place. There will be more crises before the protagonist faces the climactic action, falling action and the resolution. The story could be held together by whomever is trying to solve the case.

PLOT

It is essential for a good writer to come up with their own original plot. Avoid online plot generators at all costs. Most good plots have several key ingredients. First, you need **multiple characters with their own unique motivations**—love, revenge or money, for example. There may be several characters going after the same thing, but for different reasons. These motivations are very helpful in creating well-rounded characters. Characters with good motivations are likely to have **in-built conflicts** too. Some will be able to work together, but others won't; this will help to create tension in your story. Multiple conflicts will help to carry your plot by making it more interesting. Dropping clues and hints about what is to come in the story into the early part of your plot can also give the reader insight into your characters—this is called **foreshadowing**—and will hint at any transformation they will undergo during the course of the story.

Another subtle ploy is to use **flashbacks and flash forwards**. Flashbacks can reveal important information, showing (not telling) elements from a character's backstory. Flash forwards are equally effective, showing something that's going to happen, probably with no explanation, to build suspense.

A final recommended device is to include **recurring elements** such as motifs (for example, the mirror in *Snow White*) and symbols (the adulterous letter "A" in Nathaniel Hawthorne's *The Scarlet Letter*). These are important because they can draw storylines together, connecting actions and characters by referring to the past and the future, thus giving depth to the plot.

PLOT TEMPLATE

A useful structure that offers the writer a great deal of help is the plot template. Here's what a plot template might have looked like if Peter Benchley had drawn one up before writing *Jaws*.

Main Character
•   Martin Brody, the Chief of Police on Amity Island.

Status Quo
•   A quiet seaside town on the Atlantic coast that relies on trade from visiting tourists.

Motivation

- Brody is keen to ensure that preparations are being made to welcome tourists for the all-important summer season.

Initiating Incident

- Some swimmers are attacked by a shark, then more incidents occur and one woman is killed. Her body is washed up on the beach.

Developments

- Although the attacks continue, the mayor and local businesses put pressure on Brody not to broadcast the threat from the shark, because this will drive away the tourists and their much-needed custom. Brody calls for help, which arrives in the form of rich-kid marine biologist Matt Hooper and the local shark hunter Captain Quint. Hooper appears to be getting too close to Brody's wife.

Crisis

- Hooper confirms that the shark is a huge Great White, a deadly threat to the lives of the holidaymakers on Amity Island.

Resolution

- Although the shark puts up a good fight, killing Quint in the process, it is eventually killed.

EXERCISE: BORROWING THE SPORTSCAR

Think through a plot template, then write for 10 minutes on the following topic: Your character is a teenager and desperately wants to borrow their father's sportscar to go to a party. The teenager thinks this car will be the key to social success. Your character's father, however, says that borrowing the car is out of the question. He loves his sportscar and is convinced that the teenager will wreck it. But the teenager is not going to give up so easily....

CHAPTER SEVEN

· ·

Putting It All Together

It's Your Turn

You will have absorbed a lot of information from the pages you have read so far, and in this chapter you have the opportunity to put it all into practice by writing pieces of varying length. It would be a good idea to do them in order, not because one is easier than any other, but just because it will help your thinking process.

EXERCISE: WRITE SOME TWITTER FICTION

Tweets used to be 140 characters long, then they became 280 characters. It is a real test of a writer's skill to condense a story into a very small word limit. Give it a go, making sure you write two completely fictitious narratives. Write the first one using 140 words, then the second one using 280 words.

For this task, the word count is up to you. Write three stories, each one on a different subject. The only stipulation is that you have got just 10 minutes to write each story.

EXERCISE: TRUTH OR DARE

Write 1,000 words based on the following idea: A successful lawyer knows that his client is guilty of murder. Despite this, he believes he can easily lie to win the case, which is getting significant media coverage, and would surely guarantee that he would be made a partner at his firm.

Self-Editing

This is a good time to examine another essential part of the writing process, self-editing. If your work is going to appear in print, the publisher will usually have it copy-edited and then proofread, either in-house or by a trusted freelancer. However, this is not always the case with text that is going to appear on the internet. If articles need to go online quickly, an edit that slows down the process is an inconvenience. For this reason, some websites use text without editing it, while others put the text online and then if it gets enough hits, they "back-edit" it to ensure quality. Traditional print publishing generally insists on editing, so you should be prepared for that process.

Whatever the reason for your writing, it is essential that you self-edit your work to make sure it is as good as it can be. It is an excellent idea to review what you have written at the end of each paragraph, sentence or even phrase, as a natural part of the writing process. Some authors suggest that you end each day of writing in the middle of a sentence, to help you get going again the following session. Another way to do this is to reread what you wrote the previous day. Having had a break from writing overnight, you can review your work with fresh eyes, which will

help you perceive what you have actually written rather than what you wrote in your mind.

When you have finished writing, put your work aside for a while and let it "cook." When you come back to it, read it through completely, without changing anything. Ideally, you should read it out loud, but if you can't, read slowly and make sure you read every word. If you have trouble reading a sentence or a section, or find an issue that you want to address, just highlight it. Don't change anything now; come back to it later.

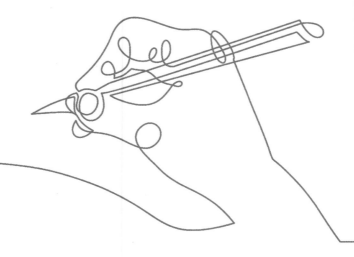

Here are some key points to watch out for:

- Coherent structure.
- Plot holes.
- Flowery language, or words that your readers might not understand. If you come across a word or phrase that jars, try looking for a synonym or use a replacement phrase.
- Limit your similes and metaphors. Many new writers overdo these, but the reader needs to understand what you are trying to say. Get rid of any mixed metaphors.
- Cut out extraneous detail and information that doesn't add to the story.
- If you're not absolutely sure of the meaning of a word you've used, look it up.
- Make sure your verb tenses match. It's a common mistake to start writing a section in the present tense, for example, then switch to the past.

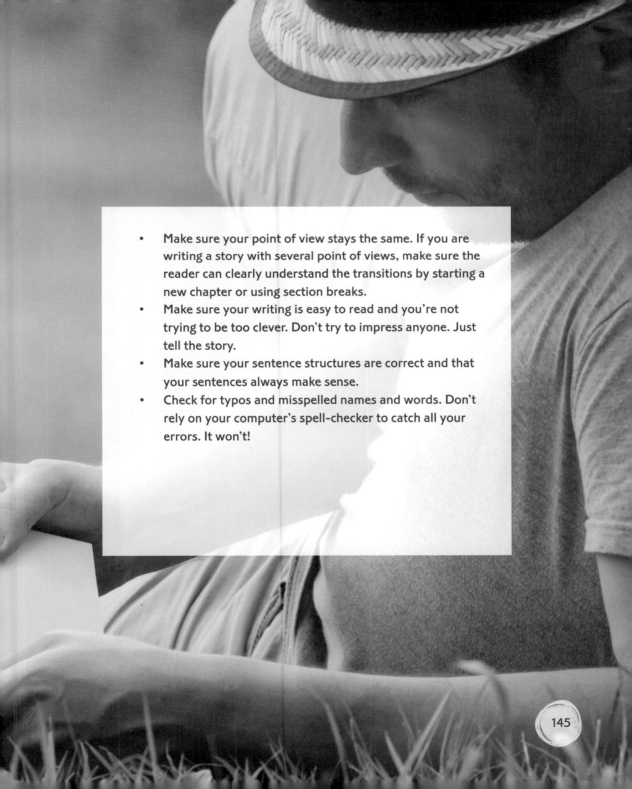

- Make sure your point of view stays the same. If you are writing a story with several point of views, make sure the reader can clearly understand the transitions by starting a new chapter or using section breaks.
- Make sure your writing is easy to read and you're not trying to be too clever. Don't try to impress anyone. Just tell the story.
- Make sure your sentence structures are correct and that your sentences always make sense.
- Check for typos and misspelled names and words. Don't rely on your computer's spell-checker to catch all your errors. It won't!

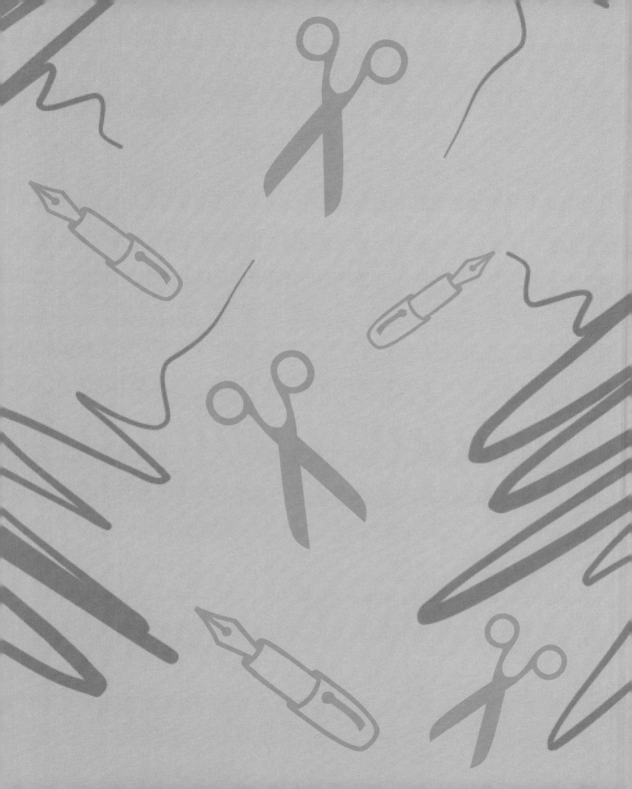

CHAPTER EIGHT

· · · · · · · · · · · · · · · · · · ·

Rule It Out

What is Good Writing?

Most people can spot the difference between a good piece of writing and a bad one. High-quality writing is approachable, interesting, and crisp; it pulls the reader along. Poor writing might have typos and grammatical mistakes, but it may also lack focus and conviction. It may have been written for the wrong audience, with a tone that doesn't match the subject. Grammatical issues are relatively easy to correct—good writers will do it naturally—but there are bigger issues to consider over and above using "effect" instead of "affect," or adding a comma when you should be using a semi-colon.

This section looks at grammar, style, and usage. All three of these elements are actually worthy of entire volumes of their own (see the recommendations on page 8); some understanding of these three facets will prepare you to write appropriately—and experience will do the rest.

Grammar

Grammar refers to the system and structure of a language, and governs how words should be combined to make sense to the reader. This section refers specifically to traditional grammar, and focuses on the distinction between what is supposedly "right" or "wrong." Interestingly, many English grammatical rules do not spring from the structure of the language or how it developed, but are actually based on Latin. Furthermore, traditional English grammar does not necessarily develop with time and contemporary usage. This is partly why the issue of grammar is so divisive, and why correct usage is often a matter of opinion rather than fact. So, grammar is important and there are many rules, but syntax is also important—that is, the arrangement of words and phrases to create well-formed sentences. Finally, you need to combine grammar and good content to write well.

One area of writing in which grammar and syntax are particularly important is dialogue, which is often idiomatic and includes incomplete sentences, slang and so on—all features that break grammatical rules. But rules are there to be broken! One such rule says that sentences should not end with a preposition. But what if someone says, "Do you know what a colporteur is?" You'll say, "No, but I'll find the dictionary and look it up," and an editor would have no problem with that.

Other rules, however—such as subject-verb agreement and the proper use of punctuation—should be respected because they are crucial for clarity and therefore very important to the meaning of your writing. A few important rules that you should adhere to are explained in the pages that follow.

Common Grammatical Mistakes

Commas: These are often overused. They should indicate to readers that they need to take a break before proceeding with the rest of the sentence, to separate an introductory word or phrase from the rest of the sentence, and to separate two clauses in a compound sentence. **Delete superfluous commas**.

Semi-colons: These should be used to separate two independent but related clauses in one sentence. Like commas, they can be used in lists, but are more useful to show bigger separations in a list. For example: "We had a reunion with family from Salt Lake City, Utah; Los Angeles, California; and Albany, New York."

Active/Passive Voice: In the active voice, the subject of the sentence performs the action (for example, "The author wrote the book"); in the passive voice, the subject receives the action (for example, "The book was written by the author"). Use the active voice UNLESS you want to emphasize the action, to be consistent, or to create an authoritative tone.

Its vs It's: "Its" is possessive; "it's" with an apostrophe is a contraction of "it is."

Your vs You're: "Your" is possessive; "you're" is a contraction of "you are."

Their vs They're vs There: "Their" is possessive; "they're" is a contraction of "they are;" "there" refers to a specific place.

I vs Me: These are both personal pronouns. Use "I" when the sentence is about you (the subject); use "me" when you are being acted upon by someone or something else (the object). Tip: If the sentence includes "you and" other people (it often does), then remove the other people, reread the sentence and you will be able to tell whether "I" or "me" is correct. For example: "Here's a picture of you and I when we went to New York," or "Here's a picture of you and me when we went to New York." Reread these without "you and," and you will quickly realize which is correct.

That vs Which: "That" is a restrictive pronoun, vital to the noun to which it refers. For example, the sentence "Baby foods that contain soya beans are best" means that foods without soya beans are inferior. In contrast, "which" introduces a relative clause, which may allow qualifiers that are not essential. For example, "The book, which I found in a dusty second-hand book shop, was a real page-turner." Remember: "that" restricts; "which" qualifies.

Could've/Should've/Would've: Some people erroneously believe that the "ve" in these words represents "of." In fact, these words are contractions of "could have," "should have" and "would have."

Style

The way in which writing is presented is referred to as "style"—this includes word choices, sentence structures, and paragraph structures. If grammar refers to what a writer does, style refers to how a writer does it. There are plenty of well-respected and exhaustive style guides that have been published for years (see the recommendations on page 8). But style is very often a preference, and writers will find that publishers each have their own preferred "house styles," which they will present to you in the form of a style guide.

Usage

Usage concerns the appropriateness of writing for our intended audience. It's the difference between, "Hello, sir. How are you today?" and "What's up, man! You doin' okay?" Both are greetings addressed to a male, followed by a question enquiring about the listener's condition. One is formal, the other is not, and they're appropriate in different scenarios. This is an important concern for writers because it can mean the difference between getting your audience's attention and alienating them.

Usage stands at the cutting edge of language because, unlike the static rules of grammar, it moves with the development of language, which can sometimes go completely against tradition. Languages—particularly English, which is spoken in more than 50 countries around the world—are incredibly diverse. As I.S. Fraser and L.M. Hodson explained in *Twenty-One Kicks at the Grammar Horse*, "Usage is trendy, arbitrary, and above all, constantly changing, like all other fashions—in clothing, music, or automobiles. Grammar is the rationale of a language, usage is the etiquette."

Write two passages of dialogue in which a parent chides their child for staying out later than intended. Set the first passage in the year 1900. Then rewrite it as though the same conversation occurred in 2019.

TOP TIPS FOR WRITERS

- Read to write.
- Writing anything is better than nothing.
- Pick the hours that work best for you.
- Don't worry about bad drafts.
- Don't drink and write.
- Avoid the TV and the internet.
- Be a bit arrogant about your work.
- Stay up late.
- Stop writing while the going is good.
- Get a cat.

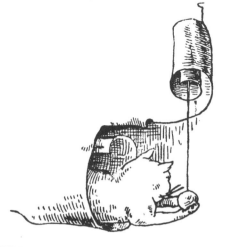

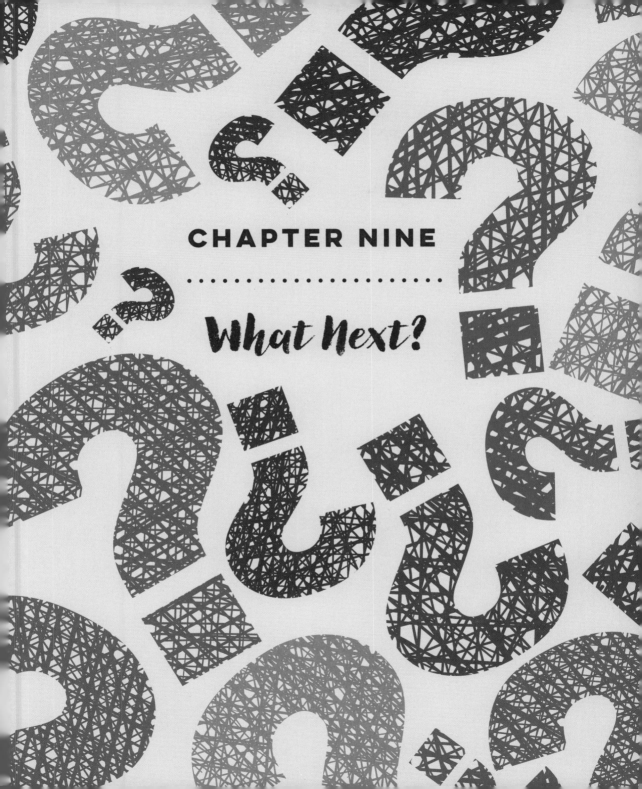

CHAPTER NINE

· · · · · · · · · · · · · · · · ·

What Next?

Do What You Wanna Do

Writing can be a solitary occupation, but once you have started to write regularly, it will be time to spread your wings. Get other people to read your work, and always listen to their comments afterwards. You could sign up for a creative writing class. This will provide you with a range of advice, writing exercises, and the motivation to write regularly. It will also give you the chance to judge yourself against others, read your work out loud, and receive honest and genuine feedback. Another alternative would be to join a book club, which will force you to read books you may not necessarily have chosen yourself, exposing you to a whole new world of writing styles.

For the writer who wants to take their work further, why not send something appropriate to a web magazine, blog or some other website? Don't expect payment—just get your stuff out there. If it gets posted, then your name will be attached and you will suddenly have a presence and a concrete addition to your portfolio. You may then be approached to write other articles on the same or different subjects. Don't ignore traditional print publications either—magazines, local newspapers, and so on still need thousands of articles to fill their pages. It may not make you rich, but it's always a thrill to see your name in print.

If you are serious about writing something more substantial, you have two choices. First, settle down in your garret room and write your book. Second, write a synopsis and a sample chapter. Whichever route you choose, it is important to note that publishers generally no longer accept unsolicited manuscripts. They simply don't have the time. Instead, you can approach a literary agent. They will read your work and give you honest, professional feedback. If they don't like what you send them, remember that writing is completely subjective and that one refusal does not mean that you can't write. Keep trying! If they do like it, they will help you in whatever way they can, advising you about the best way forward for your novel/idea/writing style and so on, and then approach the publishers they think most appropriate for you. Exhaustive lists of writers' resources, publishers, and literary agents can be found in the annual *Writers' and Artists' Yearbook*, *Writer's Market* or the *firstwriter. com* website, which are must-reads for all aspiring writers.

Thanks for reading, and good luck with your writing!